The Crystal Keys

Crystals, Devas and the Keys of Creation

Healing your crystals, yourself and the Earth in harmony with Planetary devic consciousness through the Keys of Creation

by Shabdan

Iona Light Books

The Crystal Keys

First published in March 2009
by Iona Light Books
P.O. Box 10070, Dundee DD2 5YT

www.iona-light.co.uk

Copyright © Grahame Wyllie (also known as Shabdan), 2009
All rights reserved

*Grahame Wyllie (also known as Shabdan)
is hereby identified as the author of this work.
The moral right of the author has been asserted*

No part of this publication may be reproduced, stored in a retrieval system, or transmitted, in any form or by any means, without the prior permission in writing of the publisher, nor be otherwise circulated in any form of binding or cover other than that in which it is published and without a similar condition including this condition being imposed on the subsequent publisher.

ISBN 978-0-9562069-0-9

Photographs © Shastra, cover design and book layout by Shabdan and Shastra

Contents

Introduction	1
Stories from the Crystal Realms	3
A Meeting with the Mineral Kingdom	3
Synchronicities	5
Stone Circles	6
Working with Crystals	14
Working with the Keys of Creation	15
Preparation	16
Cleansing Crystals	16
Working More Deeply with Crystals	18
Connecting with the Over-Lighting Devas of Crystals	18
Crystal Core Essence and Light-Programming your Crystals	23
Programming a Crystal	25
Meditation with Crystals	26
Healing the Crystalline You	28
Working with the Body Blueprint	28
Etheric Blueprint Body Healing	33
Side Effects, Emotional Release	36
Continuing the Work with Your Body	38
Healing the Crystalline Earth	39
A Note of Thanks	45
Appendices	46
Table 1: Cleansing, Divine Relationship, Core essence	47
Table 2: Programming and Meditating with Crystals	48
Table 3: Healing Through Your Body Etheric Blueprint	49
Table 4: Healing the Earth	51

Dedication

The Crystal Keys is dedicated to the over-lighting devas and to devic consciousness, long forgotten by humanity but without whom no life in our physically manifested world would be possible

Acknowledgements

My thanks to Seh-ruanna, who first suggested creating a book from my special evenings using the Keys of Creation to work with crystals and devic consciousness. This helped me give full attention to the subject and further develop the work that has been presented here.

Special thanks go to Shastra for her editing and proofing of The Crystal Keys, her photographs, and all of the hard work that has brought this project to fruition.

Finally, my thanks go to the clients who have worked with these energy tools and given such positive feedback.

Introduction

The Keys of Creation are a part of our inheritance from the divine. As a third dimensional awakened aspect of the Keeper of the Keys of Creation, I can access these amazing tools of alignment to the divine and express them in our world. The Keys can be manifested in the form of light language – specific phonetic phrases that invoke the energy of the Keys to complete a given task, and used extensively for the work we will undertake in this book in relation to crystalline structure. They offer incredible opportunities for healing, re-alignment and the awakening of deeper levels of consciousness to all who choose to access them.

Our crystal cousins have so much to give us. They come in an amazing array of colours, shapes and sizes, with awesome power and differing qualities, and bring us such deep Love, healing and pleasure. They offer divine service to this world – unconditional Love and unselfish action in all environments to which they are exposed.

Working with the Keys of Creation in conjunction with the over-lighting devas of Creation – an incredible part of divine consciousness that sustains all of manifested life – gives us unprecedented access to the very heart of the Mineral Kingdoms and their crystalline structures. The devas and nature spirits that look after the plants, animals and Mineral Kingdoms are one expression of the over-lighting devic consciousness on Earth. These beings are now invisible to our sight and normal senses, but this was not always the case. All life on Earth, including humanity, could not exist in this world without the manifesting and life-supporting action of devic consciousness.

This book opens the door to devic consciousness at the highest level and gives simple step-by-step techniques that harness the power of the Keys of Creation and open pathways to enable the purity of crystals to be restored. Through this work we can re-build our divine relationship with our crystals and the over-lighting devas presiding over the crystals. It takes us back to a time when we held a sacred connection with all of life, returning us to the place of the power of our own divinity.

The Crystal Keys are a bridging step to awakened consciousness where all life within the Earth sphere of consciousness can live in harmony and balance once more. Through working with these techniques you are contributing to re-creating a sacred relationship with the Devic Kingdom. This is such an important action because the devas are saddened and perplexed by our loss of connection with them and the loss of appreciation of all that they give in divine service to us, as well as the deep kinship we once held with them.

The Crystal Keys also offer techniques for accessing the blueprints of the Mineral Kingdoms and of our own bodies to enable us to re-structure crystalline form back to its natural unencumbered state, bringing healing to Mother Earth and the possibility of the return of vitality and inner health for ourselves.

We ourselves are crystalline – based on configurations of carbon-based atoms – and so we have much more in common with the crystal realms than we might initially believe. Some of the techniques in this book can be applied equally well to a quartz crystal as to the human body, and I will show you how. The only way to discover the truth of this is to experience it. I hope that you enjoy the adventure ahead with your own crystals and with your body!

I will also explain how I discovered and how I sometimes experience the mineral realms, with the thought that this may open new pathways for you to make new connections with them for yourself.

Written between the lines of this work lies a richness of divine connection for us all. There is such a special divine feeling waiting to be re-kindled within us. The techniques employed here point the way to re-building a sacred relationship with ourselves, with Source and all of life.

Shabdan, March 2009

Stories from the Crystal Realms

Since my spiritual pathway opened to me in the early nineteen nineties, I have had many encounters with the etheric planes in the natural world. I am blessed with the ability to sense and to see into these wondrous realms of consciousness that are in service to Life and support us here. I never forget that without the devas we couldn't sustain our lives in the physical plane. Their construction and nurturing of natural form gives us the plant life that sustains our bodies. Whether we are vegetarian or carnivorous, all physical life is fed from plant life that grows in soil supported by minerals from the Mineral Kingdom.

I would like to give you an introduction to the Mineral Kingdom seen from my perspective, and some of the structures of energy associated with it, before we begin to work with the Keys of Creation in conjunction with crystalline consciousness. One of the aims of this book is to deepen awareness and foster a loving connection to the rich diversity of life that sustains our own life on Mother Earth. Perhaps some of my experiences recounted here can help you find a renewed connection with them. It will also give you an opportunity to see the Keys of Creation in action and to comprehend their nature a little more fully.

A Meeting with the Mineral Kingdom

Many years ago I met a wonderful devic being on the etheric planes of consciousness from the Mineral Kingdom, called King Anud. He is a gentle and very wise being who has beautiful soft blue and green eyes. His entire being radiates a crystalline light of rainbow colours and when he comes into my energy space, I can sense his crystalline body structure and ancient being. King Anud is a master deva in divine service to the mineral consciousness present in all stones, sand, earth and crystalline forms found within our Mother Earth. I am not an expert on crystals but I have learned a great deal from King Anud about the consciousness of crystals, and he has shown me simple and yet very powerful techniques that can help us to understand and work effectively with our crystals.

King Anud first came to me when I was putting together the information and symbols related to *Ascension Reiki*, a very pure and loving energy system of Reiki healing that was brought to me by a soul brother of mine called Joseph of Aragon. As I developed the system with Joseph, he brought me new symbols and explained their nature and the power invested in them. One day, I met a beautiful being from the Nature Kingdoms called Queen Anchuvoc who showed me a symbol related to the Nature Kingdoms (the devic consciousness that supports plant and animal life) and this got me thinking about the Earth and the crystals. Soon after, King Anud softly made his presence known to me. I could feel him nearby sitting on a rock with a great cavern in the Earth behind him where many beautiful crystals were growing. He was quietly observing me, waiting for me to notice him. I feel I have to explain that these wonderful connections were quite new to me at the time – I had also recently met the Angels who had brought me a angelic symbol for Ascension Reiki, and others who were helping me to put the system together. Feeling a little overwhelmed by all of these amazing connections, I can remember thinking that I wasn't sure if I could actually see Anud or had just made him up in my mind. However, King Anud just sat waiting patiently for me to address him – to acknowledge him.

When I finally got up the courage to trust my inner sight, I spoke to him. Right away, King Anud reached out his hand to me and, as he opened it, I could see a very beautiful and delicate clear quartz crystal key. He said that this key was a key to the Mineral Kingdoms and he asked me to place it in my heart. I took the key with great reverence and did as he asked. This Key activated all of my Mineral Keys and has enabled me to reclaim that aspect of my Key consciousness.

King Anud is never far away from me. In fact he is always present with me – and you may well be feeling his gentle and loving gaze looking at you as you read this text. He never intrudes, always waiting for me to ask a question. Of course he quite often will inspire me to ask that question, without interfering in my free will! King Anud is open to you and invites you to ask him questions too. If you cannot hear the answer, ask him to get it to you somehow and trust that it will come to you somehow, through a friend, something you read, a book, a sign on the back of the bus…

Synchronicities

I have a wonderful large quartz crystal point that works with me every day. In the late nineteen nineties I remember that a client, sitting with me in my healing room at the end of the session, remarked on this crystal. She said that she couldn't help noticing it during our session and asked if she could pick it up. I said that this was fine and she took the crystal into her hands and felt all of the surfaces and key points (natural indents on the crystal surface) on the crystal. "Yes", she said. "I thought I recognised this crystal. Did you know that it used to belong to me?" I was very surprised by this because I had been given it by a crystal shop owner in exchange for an Ascension Reiki attunement a number of months before. I thought he had bought the crystal from a wholesaler. My client explained that she had held a crystal evening in her home and this crystal had been laid out for people to touch and experience. At the end of the night, she couldn't find the crystal and realised that it had 'decided to go off with someone else'. My client is a wise soul and so she released the crystal with Love, thinking that she would never see it again – and there it was in my workspace several years later!

I also had an amazing natural quartz crystal that was extremely shiny and clear in the natural shape of the top part of a skull. This crystal told me that its name was 'Arwenta', a male consciousness who said to me as an opening statement, "Don't lose me, we have important work to do!" You will note that I said that I *had* a crystal… well, it was taken from me in the theft of a rucksack from my car. You can imagine my initial shocked reaction as I realised that it was well and truly gone. After I had recomposed myself I communicated with Arwenta on the etheric and asked if he was all right. He told me that all was well. First of all he said that this was an important opportunity for me to realise that I was allowing my attention to wander and not staying present. Although I felt remorse, I was also able to encompass the bigger picture when Arwenta said to me that he had gone to do work in the local area and that I was not to worry about losing him after all. Relieved, I let go of him.

Some time later, finding myself worrying about my friend, I tuned in to Arwenta and enquired after his health. He answered me by saying that he was well and then lightly chastised me for 'buzzing' him. He said, "You must release me now and not contact me again!" – another lesson in presence and trusting in the moment! My learned friend Arwenta is a true master living in the ever-present now. He came into my life at an important time and worked with a lot of my clients. I used to see people getting really close to him and looking in awe at his incredible light and crystal clear purity. Then I would see the healing that Arwenta radiated to them, followed by a sharp intake of breath as they had to make an adjustment to their vibration. I now bless Arwenta, wherever he is in the ever-present now, and acknowledge his teachings in this world.

As I am sure you are likely to have guessed, it didn't take long for other amazing crystals to grab my attention on crystal stalls at the complementary health fairs where I sometimes work. They waited patiently for me to realise that we had already decided on the inner planes, in conjunction with my guides, that they were coming home with me if I would have them!

Stone Circles

Stone circles are evidence of ancient awareness of connections between spiritual life, crystals in the form of stones, and Mother Earth. The properties of stone circles are held in the alchemy between the stones themselves, their positioning in the landscape and their connection with the energies of the Earth, a powerful interaction between humans and the special and hidden qualities of their natural environment. While many circles today are broken and off-balance (sometimes through modern intervention in addition to the impact of the passage of time and natural decay), others are still positive and active even now, giving us access to the beautiful energies of the Earth and the universe.

On a recent holiday with two of my three children, I visited some ancient castles in the north of Scotland. On a couple of forays out in the countryside we came across two stone circles. The first was on a hillside near to Huntly,

Amethyst Geode

Gold Ray Crystal in Snow

Aberdeenshire, about a mile's walk from a minor road. Walking up to the circle we found ourselves in managed woodlands with heather and gorse growing on the open land. As we approached the circle, I at first thought that it was energetically abandoned and incomplete. However my teenage son, who had bounded ahead on his long legs, had already surveyed the site and reported that all of the stones were there and that, except for two, they had all fallen outwards. Just to be on the safe side, I asked him to come out of the area and I carefully approached the circle to check its energies.

Whenever I enter an energy structure in nature, be it a fairy dell, a woodland area off the beaten track or a stone circle, I always ask the presiding light energies or guardians if it is all right for me to approach. I know that many people, unaware of the natural energy structures and beings present in the supporting dimensions to our third dimensional consciousness, will roam freely over the countryside, letting their dogs run through the fairy dells and jump about on fallen stone circle stones. I bear them no ill will, and I know that if they could see and sense what I am privileged to experience, they too would stop and consider that it is probably appropriate to ask permission to enter these amazing places and to share in the incredible energies open within them.

This overgrown fallen circle was certainly active. Unusually in this situation, Mother Earth spoke to me and requested that I balance the circle using the Keys of Creation. I did this by intention, opening my heart chakra and linking with Source to create a pathway for divinity to bring in the necessary frequencies of light to align the stone circle to Source once again. I observed that the energy of the circle only required a minor adjustment to bring it to balance, but I was surprised to connect with Mother Earth here. Of course she is everywhere and we are within the influence of her energies all the time, but in my experience of going into stone circles, these ancient monuments are now often held by other levels of consciousness in the Earth planes which are not always working in the light. I am not used to connecting to the circles in relationship with Mother Earth, and so this, for me, was exceptional.

As I entered the circle I noticed how soft the energy was. I immediately felt other-worldly and taken into my heart. I invited my son and my daughter (also a teenager) to join me. They both took involuntary sighs and stood relaxed, focusing on the energies that they could feel there. All three of my children have long sensed spiritual energies of the light and shadow in this world. I feel so honoured to have helped bring such wonderful beings into the world and to be their father in this lifetime. They have helped me on a number of occasions to re-balance discordant energy patterns in various locations around Scotland. In these moments, when we come together in an energy space, their child consciousness steps back and an element of their master consciousness comes forward. There in that stone circle stood two very learned masters of light in not fully matured bodies, but alert and centred, absorbing the sweet vibrations that we were all experiencing in the circle. My son remarked that he could feel the change in the circle energies after I invoked the Keys and that he liked the energy better now.

I asked them to find a comfortable place to sit on the outer edges of the circle as I found myself drawn to the centre. There I was invited to sit down and connect into the heart of Mother Earth. I was blessed by Mother Earth and felt her healing energy wash over me. She asked me to bring some water into the centre of the circle, so I asked my daughter to pass me the small bottle of water we had with us. I sat holding the water bottle quietly in my hands, not knowing what to expect. After a short time I noticed that there was a beautiful energy coming through my hands and the water was absolutely radiant with white light. My first thought was that Mother Earth was simply blessing the water but I soon realised that this powerful energy-charging of the water was more than just that. After a time the energy flow stopped and Mother Earth told me that she had blessed the water deeply and that its vibration was now sacred. She explained that a teaspoon could be taken and put into another bottle of water and that the second bottle would take on the blessed properties of this first one. I could already feel the beautiful vibrations of the water in my hand and was absolutely delighted!

I sat gratefully in the circle centre as Mother Earth invited my children into the centre of the circle to join me. She then began to bring us all healing energy. They both had powerful experiences. My son told me that he felt a profound shift and had cleared some deep-set energy blocks that had been troubling him for some time. My daughter's elfin energy side was shining softly and she seemed to merge with the bracken and grassland around her. She simply curled up and went to sleep, looking radiant and serene. I too felt an incredible release and let go a great deal, moving my spiritual vibration on to a new level. Since that day, my hay fever symptoms have fallen away from the debilitating allergy I have suffered all of my life to a mild problem.

On the following day we three highland 'musketeers' came across another circle which we had driven all over the place along back roads to reach. All of the signs seemed to point in the right direction but never quite took us there. I was beginning to doubt the validity of chasing after this circle any further and thought perhaps someone was attempting to tell me something. Just as I was about to turn back, we drove onto a narrow road with passing places. Now committed to following the road, we came across a turning that led to the circle. Being there, it seemed churlish to not go to the stones so we ambled up the track towards the circle. I got my first warning sign some fifty metres from the circle and asked my children to stop the light-hearted chattering that we were enjoying together and allow me to go first. Soon they too noticed the heavy energy and fell in behind me, walking out of their teenage selves and more into their master energy.

When we arrived at the stones I was surprised to see a complete circle, every stone weathered and rough-hewn, but intact. This circle is known as the Recumbent Circle on account of the large recumbent stone that is shouldered by two upright stones on either side. Archaeologists believe that the recumbent stone was used to observe the stars and gather data about the heavens, but to me it looked more like an altar stone.

I approached quietly and observed the energies at work. I noticed two sets of guardians of the circle. One set, standing back, were light and clear in their vibration. The other set, who were to the fore, seemed less clear. I suddenly saw with my etheric awareness a large quartz crystal skull gleaming from the centre of the circle and surmised that one had been brought into the space and worked with there. I approached the lighter of the two sets of guardians and asked if I could enter the circle. Although I asked this, I had no intention of entering the circle with the energies that I could sense within its perimeter. The light guardians explained that the lesser vibration beings had been introduced into the circle by people visiting the site and were not the true guardians of this site. They asked me to use the Keys and to release these others into the light. The energy work I undertook with the Keys, which always work under grace, never interfering in free will, was quite substantial and after a period of time, and several deep shudders to the bone later, I completed the work and felt it was all right to enter the circle.

As the energy of the now re-balanced circle settled down, I could feel the perfect energy form of a complete circle around me. I asked my children to stay outside the circle as I explored the energies, making sure that there were no low vibration energy surprises waiting to overlay their vibrations on mine, and then I invited them into the circle. My son, tall warrior, full of zest for life, forged ahead and wandered amongst the stones. My daughter, with her elfin gentleness, hesitated and chose to remain outside. I felt drawn to sit at the centre of the circle and then realised that further Keys could be used to strengthen the light energy balance of the circle more fully. After this my daughter felt comfortable to enter the circle and chose one of the standing stones to prop herself against.

One of the interesting attributes of this circle was described on an information board positioned on the path before we entered the site itself. It cryptically explained that the circle was understood to have unique sound characteristics and so, sitting at the centre of the circle, I began to tone softly towards the recumbent stone. Toning is a way of making a resonant vocal sound that is pure and unadorned by vibrato. Its simple vibration has powerful healing properties that can correct energy imbalances in a physical body or in a room or space. As I made several tones I was aware of the sound coming out of my mouth and acoustically travelling around me in the familiar way, but in addition to this the sound was bouncing off the stones and resonating quite powerfully around the circle space. I was amazed by this resonance. I was making this sound in the open air in a fairly large stone circle space, and although there was no wind to carry the sound waves away from me, there was equally little to reflect them back to me. Both my children noticed the effect and they said that the sound appeared to be coming from all around the circle and was quite loud even though they were a distance away from me.

King Anud explained that the stone circle had been constructed so that when sound vibrations resonate into the stones, the frequency tuning of the circle causes them to reflect back out into the circle space. He explained that this circle could radiate sound waves deeply into the core of Mother Earth and bring focused healing waves to wherever the energy was directed. This is of course one of the ways that we can work with our own crystals once they have been fully cleansed and balanced. Crystals can amplify and direct sacred intention through sound. Sound healing is beyond the scope of this book, but the initial steps to prepare yourself and your crystals for this and any other kind of healing are described in the chapters that follow.

In our human ignorance, when we lost our connection with the natural world to a greater extent as we moved away from our hearts into our minds, we discarded a rich and vital heritage. The Mineral Kingdom devas (and those who support the land and plant life) are deeply affected by the discordance that pervades stone circles these days. The energy corrections that I, and others, make to these structures are important. In balancing their energies we enable the circle energies to radiate light vibrations into the natural world around the circle. This in turn has a positive influence on humanity as well as nature. In all experiences that I have in the countryside, I can feel Spirit and Mother Nature gently guiding me, inspiring me to re-activate our divine relationship and to bring back harmony between us once more.

I never go out of my way looking for things to do, but since there are no real boundaries between our human world, the devic kingdoms and our living, breathing Mother Earth, and as I step ever more deeply into a natural relationship with our complete world, it is easy for me to bring the Keys to bear on a given situation and restore balance within the system.

As I write this, I am aware of King Anud in his crystal chamber sitting with me. He speaks to me softly in my heart and thanks me for sharing these simple stories. He tells me of a time when humanity and the devas walked hand in hand and shared life and stewardship of this planet together. "Those were such rich days, my friend. I could sit here long enough and tell tales to kindle a warmth in your heart that opens your consciousness to our divine relationship. Ah, Shabdan, blessed be!"

I think that I will sit here and listen to King Anud for a while. While I do so, perhaps you can read on and discover this wonderful relationship through *The Crystal Keys!*

Working with Crystals

Crystals offer a profound connection to the natural world and the inner realms of higher consciousness. They are filled with amazing faces, colours, rainbows and structures that can change and respond to our loving touch and attention. A cloudy crystal can clear and become radiant and shiny through repeated loving care and touching. Rainbows can appear within a lacklustre crystal simply through it being given attention. Many people are drawn to crystals because of their colours, incredible form and appearance. We often buy crystals because of a 'special feeling' we experience in response to seeing and touching a crystal in a shop display or at a healing fair. We take them home and unwrap them with excitement, stroke them or hold them to the heart chakra. We feel their beautiful vibration and drift off into a meditative state, breathe and sigh, and after some time gently place the crystal on a shelf or in a cabinet and… there it can stay for weeks, months or even years.

Of course, not everyone will do this, but I know that many people who are drawn to certain crystals and are building an increasingly large collection of them are a little perplexed about how to relate and work with them. Some people have said to me that they feel afraid to handle their crystals or feel insecure about interacting with them. If you do work with your crystals, do you know how to awaken their divine being and reconnect them to the mineral consciousness and their original purpose so that they can offer their highest contribution to the world? I'd like to take you through a simple process with your crystals to bring you into *divine relationship* with them and to help them give their beautiful best to the world.

I think the most important thing to remember about the crystals we are so lucky to have found is that they are going to be with us for a very short time in relation to their overall life span. They are mineral beings and are likely to exist for thousands of years or even longer. We can be no more than temporary guardians to them. I think this is a profoundly important point to remember. Treat them with loving respect and allow them to reveal to you their divine gifts - and be prepared to let them circulate in the world according to their heart's guidance. Don't hold on to them simply because you are attached to them or because you want to own a beautiful crystal collection.

> Perhaps now is a good time to review your collection of crystals and either sell on the ones that you haven't looked at for a long time, or pass them on with love, intuitively choosing the recipient so that the crystal can bring its heart energies once again to act for the highest good in this world.

Working with the Keys of Creation

Before beginning any of the following work, please take time to read through all the information and instructions to familiarise yourself with the processes so that you can hold your attention easily on the purpose of each Anaritas phrase and action. With a little practice, the process becomes really easy to undertake each time.

Some of the following Anaritas light language and instruction has come from King Anud. It is designed to be used in conjunction with the Keys of Creation to help you to work more deeply with your crystals. The Keys of Creation appear in several forms, either as symbols, light language or in the form of metaphysical Keys that can be invoked to balance and heal. The Anaritas light language is simply the expression of the Keys in phonetic-sound form. The Keys open a pathway to create alignment to the divine within the energy system or structure they have been invoked to serve. When you say the phrases below out loud, the sound resonance opens a pathway from the Keys (which come directly from Source with no intermediate steps). The energy comes into the crystals and into you to create a divine balance within the crystal and within you. The Keys are very powerful, and the invocation of the light language always works if the phrases are spoken with intention. In addition, the Keys always work under the Law of Grace and do not interfere in free will. Only in exceptional circumstances is it possible to prevent the Keys from working for you and this is likely to happen in the form of self-sabotage, where fear prevents healing and alignment to the divine.

Preparation

Before using the Anaritas phrases in any of the healing tools in this book, it is wise to centre and ground yourself thoroughly. Grounding can be done using these Anaritas phrases. Begin by saying these first phrases softly out loud with the intention of achieving what is described in the bracketed description:

Secu-narimbido [Spoken: secoo-narim-beedoh]
Take a deep breath and release, let go...
(Aligns your spiritual essence to the physical body)

Secu-ambido-nos [Spoken: secoo-am-beedoh-noss]
Take a deep breath and release, let go...
(Releases self-sabotage or psychological reversal)

Garusan [Spoken: garoosan]
(Grounds the physical body and spirit into the heart of Mother Earth)

(Take a deep breath and let go after saying each phrase)

Cleansing Crystals

It is important to cleanse crystals regularly. Crystals always naturally serve their environment and will absorb as much as they can of discordant frequencies and then work to transform them. Small crystals can only take on a little energy before they get overloaded and are unable to help you any more. For example, rings with diamond or other stone settings cannot absorb very much low vibration energy because of their size, but their light qualities can be very positive and helpful to you. If you are going to wear them, cleanse them before you put them on and if during the day you have an argument with someone or get upset and tearful, or if you find yourself in a heavy energy environment, remember to use the Anaritas cleansing phrase to cleanse them. It will only take half a minute or so and then the stone can help you effectively once again.

Any crystal that has not been worked with for a period of time is constantly absorbing discordant frequencies from its environment and will become energetically dirty. Before undertaking any work with crystals it is important to cleanse them. I cleanse my crystals every time I pick them up to use. I find this particularly important in working with my clients. It ensures that the crystals are completely clear and in balance, and hence able to work effectively and bring no discordant energy to my clients.

Instructions

Centre and ground yourself, bringing your mind to stillness and moving your attention into your heart chakra. Hold your crystal in your hands. Say the phrase out loud to the crystal. Then take a deep breath on behalf of the crystal and let go. Continue to hold the crystal for as long as you feel the crystal needs you to after saying the phrase, loving and supporting your crystal as you do so. This will really help the crystal to cleanse deeply and to be nurtured by the Mineral Kingdom. If you pay close attention to your crystal, you will feel it opening up and almost sighing and relaxing!

Say the phrase below out loud with sacred intention over the crystal, which you hold in your right hand. *(If the crystal you are working with is too big or too heavy to hold in your hands, place both of your hands on the crystal. When placing your hands on a large crystal, don't splay out your fingers to try and cover a larger area of the crystal. Keep your fingers together. This allows the energy to transmit more effectively through your hands to the crystal.)*

Veh-Reh-Shua, Eh-San, Eh-San

This phrase deeply cleanses negativity and brings Love and nurture to a crystal. The Anaritas phrase can be repeated up to three times (if necessary) to fully cleanse a crystal.

> *Remember that crystals can take on too much, just like you can. When they are overloaded, their energy is blocked and they cannot function. Cleanse them regularly so that they can give loving service to you and to the world.*

Further Cleansing...

Crystals love moonlight, which can re-charge them. When the moon is bright, or at the full moon, place them on a windowsill overnight and let them soak up the beautiful moonlight. You will feel the difference in the morning.

Important: remember that some crystals will bleach in direct sunlight so don't forget to retrieve them in the morning.

Cleanse crystal/mineral pendants and rings every day before wearing them. If you encounter a dense energy environment, cleanse the crystals again to help them to continue working effectively with you.

Crystals love to be handled. In some ways they are like children and require nurturing, talking and listening to. They can become traumatised if placed under too much pressure or asked to cope with powerful emotional energy. If one of your crystals becomes dull and lifeless, cleanse it thoroughly, giving it a lot of loving attention and caressing. Use the Anaritas light language phrases below with the crystal. If it still seems overwhelmed, seek competent professional help to heal your crystal.

Working More Deeply with Crystals

Connecting with the Over-Lighting Devas of Crystals

This step needs to be carried out individually with each crystal that you would like to harmonise your vibration with and form a divine relationship with. It need only be carried out once with each crystal but you may feel the need to repeat the step with a specific crystal if you have not worked with it for some time. This can help you to renew your connection and to remember the beautiful divine relationship that awaits your unconditional Love and attention.

Quartz Point Reflecting Nature

Baltic Amber

As we surrender ever more deeply to divine will, we learn to accept that all is perfect and all is always in divine order. The devic energies are a life-supporting consciousness, essential to all levels of life throughout Creation. Every crystal, every plant and other living being on Earth is under the care of the over-lighting devic energies. Connecting and working with the over-lighting devic energies of your crystal creates a divine pathway for the perfect expression of 'Life serving Life' in relation to you working with your crystal.

The over-lighting devas are not incarnate within the Earth planes. They are the purest expression of the devic energies that sustain all life within manifested Creation, from the quantum to the macrocosm. Part of the myriad structures of manifested Creation, they are a different strand of Creation-energy to our spiritual form and being. They do not possess free will, but serve out of pure Love for life, always giving unconditionally from their pristine loving hearts. Their frequencies interpret and translate the constantly-manifesting life-supporting energy matrices that weave the web of manifested form coming from Source.

The idea of Life serving Life is as old as Creation itself. It comes from the surrendering of self-will to divine will. In the end we will return to Source, uniting with all other separate elements of life as we do so. To achieve this, the mind that is living unconsciously will become conscious once more as unconditional Love dissolves all fear. The dissolution of fear enables the separate self to begin to unite with all that is. As it does so, it is enveloped with such Love for life that all the enlightened spirit wants to do is give out that Love and serve all of life unconditionally. Devic consciousness serves all life unconditionally in this way and the Anaritas work we are about to undertake helps us to come into a sacred loving relationship with the devic consciousness and with our crystals, which also serve life unconditionally.

The Anaritas light language that follows connects and aligns you to the specific devic over-lighting being that over-lights the crystal you are going to work with. In this work, the entire energy system comprising you, devic consciousness and crystalline structure is encompassed. We are not separate elements of human, deva and crystal. We may perceive life in that way, but energetically we are like cinematic projections on a screen. Only on the screen does the light coming from the projector bulb (one light) appear to compose the separate elements. Our separated consciousnesses of human, deva and crystal are encompassed in this work and brought into a state of unity through the invocation we make using the light language. The elements of the system are brought to one. Your loving action through the Anaritas phrases described in this section brings you to a place where you too serve life unconditionally alongside the devic and crystalline consciousness. This is a most sacred act and I ask you to take the step with gentleness in your heart and an appreciation of the nature of your action.

Instructions

Hold the crystal in your hands and centre yourself. Take time to allow yourself to come to a place of deep stillness within and a place of sacred acceptance of the divine. Use your breath to help you to let go of thoughts, tension, emotions. Let your attention rest on your heart chakra and become as present as you can – be in the now moment.

Say this phrase out loud with sacred intention over the crystal in your hands. *(If the crystal you are working with is too big or too heavy to hold in your hands, place both of your hands on the crystal)*

Shek-An, Keh-Halla-An

Meh-Sha, Uurra-An

This phrase creates a divine relationship between you, your crystal and the over-lighting deva of your crystal, establishing a loving trinity with light cords between you (a uniting action).

Breathe deeply and surrender. Become one with the devic over-lighting energies and with your crystal. Allow a sacred relationship to form between you, your crystal and the over-lighting deva. Remember that you have made a powerful invocation, inviting in the life-supporting energies of Creation to work with you. Lovingly hold your attention on the deva and your crystal for a while until you feel that the sacred connection is complete.

You may sense/feel the halo of loving light that comes to surround you and separately to surround your crystal. At this point a light cord runs between you and your crystal. From this moment onwards you are linked with the devic over-lighting energies of the crystal and with your crystal itself.

When working with your crystal, remember the over-lighting devic energies connected to it. Always work in accordance with divine will in relation to the crystal. In this way both you and the crystal can bring divine service to the world in all that you do together.

Crystal Core Essence and Light-Programming your Crystals

This step can be carried out from time to time when you work with your crystals. They will really appreciate the liberation of their energies and the renewal of a deep connection with the essence of their being and with the Mineral Kingdoms.

Crystals will accept light programmes to carry out certain tasks for you. However, it can be much more effective to programme crystals in accordance with the divine will of the crystal itself and the devic energies over-lighting the crystal.

The following Anaritas light language phrases assist the crystal in communing deeply with the Mineral Kingdoms and in 'remembering' its root nature and core consciousness.

Instructions

Hold the crystal in your hand and move into your heart and centre yourself, becoming still and present. When carrying out this two-part process, allow enough time for the crystal to re-align itself to its natural core essence state, to commune properly, receive divine blessing from the Mineral Kingdoms and to complete the process that you have invoked through the Keys of Creation.

Say the following phrases out loud with sacred intention over the crystal in your hands. *(If the crystal you are working with is too big or too heavy to hold in your hands, place both of your hands on the crystal.)*

Varishar-An, Ney-At, Ku-Rashua-An-At

Kereh-Halla-An, Eh-San, Eh-San

"Commune with the soul of your being, revive and heal. In this moment you receive the blessing of the Mineral Kingdom. And So It Is."

Kreh-Halla-An, Cru-Ak, Eh-San

Kuru-Shella-An, Eh-San, Eh-San

"Reveal the core essence of your being, and let it shine forth across all dimensions, times, planes and levels in this world. And So It Is."

When choosing to add light programmes to your crystal, work intuitively and ask for the guidance of the over-lighting deva holding the crystal. Feel the deva deeply in your heart and trust the inner guidance it brings. In this way you are acting in accordance with divine will and you will be able to bring forward the highest level of energies from your crystal with full support from the Mineral Kingdoms and the devic energies in Creation.

Programming a Crystal

It is possible to add light programmes to your crystals to support you in your healing work and spiritual unfoldment. For the most part the fact that you felt drawn to the crystals in your care – and having now created a divine relationship with them and enabled them to access their core essence and nature - it is likely that they will be able to serve you well just as they are. However, you may wish to add loving programmes to keep a space safe to meditate or work within, to bring deep illumination to you and so on.

Please bear in mind that you have come into divine relationship with your crystal. Let your heart guide you in the choice of programmes that you add. Do not place a programme within a crystal that it cannot hold or that causes it to be uncomfortable. Just because we cannot easily feel what our crystals are feeling doesn't mean that they are not experiencing life and having feelings. Remember that they are a part of the rich matrix of life to which you also belong. Having come to this new level of understanding through the work that we are doing together in this book, treat your crystals with deep loving respect for the wonderful gifts that they can bring to you and the world.

Instructions

Use this Anaritas light language phrase to assist you in adding a light programme to your crystal. Centre yourself. Hold the crystal in your hands. Say the phrase followed by the programme, then complete the phrase:

Varu-Ka-An, "programme", Eh-San, Eh-San

Please see the next page for examples of light programmes, or tune in to create your own.

Example Programmes:

1. "Hold and anchor a protection matrix to exclude low vibration discordant energy."

Varu-Ka-An "hold and anchor a protection matrix to exclude low vibration discordant energy" Eh-San, Eh-San

Choose suitable crystals that are willing and able to support the programme. You could do this particular programme with four similar quartz crystal points and place them in a square on the ground in the corners of a room or a space to hold a powerful protection matrix to exclude low vibration energies. Once you have placed the crystal points on the floor, link them by loving intention to create a cubic grid structure that you imagine protecting the space.

2. "Open a pathway for divine Love to flow."

Varu-Ka-An "open a pathway for divine Love to flow" Eh-San, Eh-San

You can place this programme in many different kinds of crystal. When you hold the crystal in your hands and place it on a chakra or on a blocked energy place on your body you will feel a beautiful loving pathway to the divine opening up and bringing in unconditional Love.

You can choose any programme that feels appropriate to you and to your chosen crystal.

Meditation with Crystals

Crystals are wonderful meditation companions who can amplify and extend a meditation. Meditating on a particular crystal itself can offer you deep insights into the crystalline world and bring wisdom and richness to your life. You can use Anaritas light language to help you to meditate with your crystals.

The following phrase builds on the sacred relationship that you have created with your crystal. It opens a pathway between you, your crystal and the overlighting deva to open gateways to crystalline consciousness and unconditional Love, uniting you with aspects of Source.

Instructions

Choose one of your crystals that you feel drawn to meditate with. Cleanse it and ensure that you have carried out the alignment steps above, and feel that you still hold a loving relationship with it. If you feel that the connection is not clear and strong, you can take a moment to repeat all of the alignment steps to bring yourself into divine relationship with the crystal once again.

As before, say this phrase with sacred loving intention over the crystal in your hands. *(If the crystal you are working with is too big or too heavy to hold in your hands, place both of your hands on the crystal.)*

Acra-An-Nu, Sharac-Anash-An-Nu

This phrase opens a pathway between you, your crystal and the overlighting deva of your crystal to open gateways to crystalline consciousness and unconditional Love, uniting you with aspects of Source for meditation and illumination

Take a deep breath and let go.

Feel yourself uniting with your crystal and relax deeply. Allow the Anaritas light language Keys of Creation to open divine pathways within you in relation to your crystal and follow the impetus of your crystal as it guides you into meditation. Alternatively, carry out a meditation in any appropriate way that is familiar and comfortable to you with your crystal.

Healing the Crystalline You

Working with the Body Blueprint

The work that we have done so far is truly remarkable. It is a sacred union of the divine elements of crystal, deva and you. Perhaps even more remarkable is to be able to use this powerful crystalline alignment to bring profound healing to your physical body. The body is made up of a carbon-based molecular structure and can therefore be seen as crystalline in nature. This enables us to apply what we have used with our cherished crystals on our physical body too. Cleansing and balancing our physical body crystalline structure, creating a divine relationship with each and every atom and molecule of the body that we inhabit and enabling this crystal matrix to function as purely as possible in accordance with its natural pattern gives us the potential to bring our body into balance with the spiritual work and growth that we undertake on our spiritual journey.

Step 1

NOTE: for full information and detailed explanation of these steps, please refer to pages 14 and following.

Now we will go through all the light language steps to cleanse the crystal matrix of our physical body, create a divine connection and relationship with the body, nurture and heal each and every crystal structure in the body and enable it to express its root energy pattern.

Begin by grounding. Say out loud:

Secu-narimbido	*Take a deep breath and release, let go…*
Secu-ambido-nos	*Take a deep breath and release, let go…*
Garusan	*Take a deep breath and let go…*

Now place the palms of your hands over your heart chakra and over the navel (there is a main chakra behind the navel). Make sure that on both hands your fingers lie close together and the thumb is laid alongside the index finger.

Seraphim Crystal Pyramid

Divine Joy Crystal

Seraphim Spheres in Sunlight

With sacred loving intention, say the following four sets of phrases out loud to your physical body, allowing enough time at each step for the body crystalline matrix to make all of the alignments necessary:

1.   Veh-Reh-Shua, Eh-San, Eh-San

Deeply cleanses negativity, brings Love and nurtures the crystalline matrix of your body. Can be repeated up to three times if necessary to fully cleanse your body crystal matrix.

2.   Shek-An, Keh-Halla-An

Meh-Sha, Uurra-An

Creates a divine relationship between you, your crystalline body and the over-lighting deva of your crystalline structure, creating a loving trinity with light cords between you.

3.   Varishar-An, Ney-At

   Ku-Rashua-An-At

   Kereh-Halla-An, Eh-San, Eh-San

"Commune with the soul of your body crystalline being, revive and heal. In this moment you receive the blessing of the Mineral Kingdom.
And So It Is."

4.   Kreh-Halla-An, Cru-Ak, Eh-San

   Kuru-Shella-An, Eh-San, Eh-San

"Reveal the core essence of your body's crystalline being, and let it shine forth across all dimensions, times, planes and levels in this world. And So It Is."

Step 2

Having created the sacred alignment and relationship between your crystalline body, the over-lighting deva and the essence or spirit (*of you*), you can now add amazing light programmes to your physical body that are natural for the body. This can help to create the possibility of perfect health and well-being, and establish a natural energy balance that is in perfect harmony with the divine.

NOTE:

Achieving full health depends on many factors, but you may be able to do it more easily through the use of this light language. However, it is helpful to understand that prolonged ill-health or deep-set disease and disabilities are the result of multiple limiting mind patterns, thought programmes and emotions that have been laid into the body over an extended period of time in this lifetime, with possible roots buried in a series of other lifetimes. The overlaid patterns from other lifetimes can be profound in their effect and you may not have uncovered all of the aspects of fear-based emotion that are affecting your body. If any of the elements described here are continuing to influence your body, the Anaritas language will have a limited effect on your body, depending upon the severity of the emotional patterning, until you have healed the overlaid patterns.

It is always important to clear emotion affecting your body – and this may have wider repercussions that affect your mental well-being as well.

Another important factor is the level of commitment and focus that you give to healing the body through this technique. Your body is composed of manifested divine intention modified and overlaid by the thought forms of an unconscious mind. Consistent application of this light language work will manipulate the energy patterns that govern your manifested physical body. You must undertake this work at a greater level of intensity than that with which your mind applies and holds negative thought patterns and fear structures and you must be present enough to break free from the old mind patterns. Ten minutes good work with the Anaritas phrases followed by a day's worth of unworthy, unloving thoughts applied to your body together with continuing limiting body belief systems will substantially undermine the possible effects of the healing work on your body. Work to see it as part of a holistic healing programme of positive action and thought in which you set the intention to observe, identify and restructure all negative thought forms and patterning in order to support your healing.

This technique has a remarkable potential for healing your body and is well worth the diligent application necessary to improve your physical health and well-being. The process contributes to achieving greater levels of presence in your life – a fundamental state of spiritual being.

Etheric Blueprint Body Healing

You have an etheric blueprint upon which the form and structure of your body is based. If left to follow that blueprint uninterrupted, the body can easily adopt a natural pattern of health and well-being. What interrupts the continuing adoption of the perfect form of the etheric blueprint? It is the unconscious *you,* which encompasses all mind-level emotion, issues and fear, all belief systems and the life environment and situations you have created that lead you to adopt the patterns of fear that you currently hold. This includes patterns from all other lifetimes where the unhealed attitudes and fears of those lifetimes have been imprinted into your body. This combined patterning is often overlaid upon the physical body because we cannot deal with the torment, stress and fear that has come to overwhelm us. We often use our bodies as receptacles or storage vessels for all of our unhealed emotion. As we know, if left in the body for too long, ignored and suppressed, these emotions can develop into acute pain that can lead to deep-set body discomfort and eventually disease.

Instructions

Using the following technique and Anaritas language you can work to release the overlaid energy patterns and guide the body back towards its original and natural healthy form.

1. Begin by clearing and balancing the etheric blueprint so that it is able to hold its perfect form. This ensures that any subsequent programming work carried out in accordance with the etheric blueprint is going to be pure and in proper alignment to the divine. The etheric blueprint can be cleansed either by asking the angels to cleanse and heal it for you or by using the following Anaritas phrase which will address the blueprint directly and bring it into perfect alignment with the divine, cleansing and balancing it as it does so.

   Say the following phrase softly out loud, sending the intention of the phrase to your etheric blueprint:

   Sherak-Ka-Han, Shellath, Sherat

   Ah-Han, Han-Nu

   Take a deep breath and let go. Allow a short time for the etheric blueprint to cleanse, repair and come into balance.

2. Now gently hold awareness of the beautiful over-lighting deva who oversees your physical body's crystalline structure standing in front of you and sending loving devic life-support energy to you.

3. At the same time, hold awareness of your etheric blueprint surrounding your physical body. Your intention is to direct the over-lighting devic life-sustaining energies of Creation through your etheric blueprint and allow this incredible light pattern to shine onto and through your physical body, deep into every crystalline molecular structure that forms your body. In this way you are gently re-programming your body in accordance with divine will, enabling it to adopt the patterning of perfect form and beingness.

To activate and sustain the over-lighting devic energies shining through your etheric blueprint into your physical body, use the following Anaritas phrase:

Arass, Cru-Ak, Kerrah-Alla-An

Eh-San, Eh-San

Feel the life-sustaining patterns radiating into your physical body through the etheric blueprint. Feel the involvement of the over-lighting devas invoked through the Keys of Creation in Anaritas light language form.

Visualise this actually happening. 'See' the beautiful and extremely high vibration divine light of the over-lighting devic energy shining brightly through the etheric blueprint and visualise this soft soothing light radiating deeply into your body tissue, molecules and crystalline structure. Then say:

Meh-ha-ta, Seh-An, Seh-An

Breathe and release...

This phrase temporarily releases the emotional overlays that your torment and fear have layered into your physical body to allow the natural re-patterning of the etheric blueprint light structure to reach deeply into the crystalline structure of the physical body, uninterrupted by emotional and belief-system overlays, whilst the energy work is taking place.

The phrase works by temporarily lifting all emotional overlays that you have placed in your body. It does not disconnect them - it simply releases them from the body to enable the body to experience itself uninhibited by emotion. The duration of the phrase's effect is determined by the intensity of the emotion you have layered into your physical body. If the emotional overlay is great, the phrase's effect will last for only a number of seconds. However, this will be long enough to enable the first part of the mantra to reach into the cellular and crystalline structure of the body. In this way, the new programming from the etheric blueprint is more likely to be sustained within the crystalline structure after you stop repeating the mantra.

Now repeat the two phrases as a mantra:

Arass, Cru-Ak, Kerrah-Alla-An
Eh-San, Eh-San

Meh-ha-ta, Seh-An, Seh-An

- continue to repeat the mantra, breathing after each phrase. Do this slowly and gently with deep awareness of the sacred process of reprogramming that you are bringing to your physical body. You need to be present and fully engaged in the process to achieve maximum results
- As you repeat the mantra, remember the sacred relationship you have invoked through the crystal Anaritas phrases that harmonise you with your body, the over-lighting deva, the Mineral Kingdoms and the essence of you (the one reading this text, who understands and experiences the sacred relationship – the *real* you)
- Do your best to remain in your heart and connected to the process you are undertaking
- Repeat the phrases for a comfortable period of time, using your discernment to guide you

Side Effects, Emotional Release…

It is possible that you will experience emotional release for a period of time after working with this mantra. This is a release of the emotional overlays that you originally placed into your body and that are now being displaced as the body attempts to re-adopt its natural healthy form. You may also find that, having disturbed the equilibrium of an uneasy emotional truce (involving the holding of emotion anchored in your body), you need to address the issues that arise through the blueprint work. The body emotional release may be accompanied by a level of physical toxin release as the build-up of chemicals stored in your body by the emotional issues (that the body was inhibited from releasing before) is now released. To avoid discomfort in your body, **please drink enough good quality water** (bottled low-mineral content water is often the best) to flush through your body and successfully release the toxins in your bloodstream.

PLEASE REMEMBER THAT EXCESSIVE USE OF THE MANTRA CAN LEAD TO A HEALING CRISIS IN YOUR PHYSICAL BODY *AND* BRING ABOUT EMOTIONAL TRAUMA AS YOU PROCESS WHAT YOU HAVE BEEN HOLDING IN YOUR BODY

If you programme your body too quickly to adopt a healthy natural pattern, it will respond by attempting to re-align itself to a natural state of health and balance more quickly than you are able to process the side-effects of the readjustment, and this is likely to cause a substantial toxin release into the blood stream, giving you that tired, hung-over feeling.

It is also possible that you will experience excessive emotional trauma as your body, now beginning to follow a pattern of natural health, begins to reject the emotional overlays that have suppressed its natural function. Of course, another consequence of working too intensively is the risk of psychological reversal, a state of self sabotage where the emotional shift is too great and causes a panic within the fear-filled parts of you that will then completely reject the positive benefits of the good work that you have done.

It is far better to undertake this work gradually and consistently on a daily basis rather than doing a major self-healing session on one or two days.

Continuing the Work with Your Body

It is important to understand that the physical body is the densest medium of our inhabitation within the Earth planes. It is often the last dumping ground for our unhealed emotion – the deepest of fears and terror that we are unable to address and release. Most of us have spent a lifetime or lifetimes layering up the emotion into our bodies through an incredible level of repeated fear-filled thoughts, trauma, shock and terror-filled experiences, from little heart-stopping moments to the greater traumas of accidents, emotional overload, bereavement, violence, wars, and so on. In addition, we carry the overlay of emotion from the many levels of collective consciousness of which we are a part within the Earth sphere of consciousness. Therefore working to change your body for the better, releasing the trapped emotion and transforming a dysfunctional or diseased physical body – the densest element of your being – can take time.

The Anaritas language brings you more deeply into divine relationship with Creation and with the over-lighting devas with each recital of the phrasing. This work re-programmes your physical body through your etheric blueprint and it will cause subtle changes to take place within the body that can lead to a higher level of function within. This will encourage a recovery of the body's function and offer the opportunity for an improved level of health.

Repeat this work regularly at a sensible and practical rate to bring about significant and permanent beneficial changes in your physical body health and well-being, and in your energy levels.

I cannot prove any of what I have written in *The Crystal Keys* scientifically. However, with the great leaps of discovery now taking place within quantum physics, it is quite possible that the scientific evidence is waiting just around the corner to be discovered. Some quantum physicists already know that our world is a thought world and that you can change things through changing your thinking. If this is true, then your thinking, both positive and negative, is already affecting your body. The positive intentions that I have invested in this coding for pure expression of consciousness within the physical planes can only encourage a higher, purer expression of your consciousness through a body that is less inhibited by restrictive physical patterns. As you believe, so you create. Believe in yourself and in healing your body through your etheric blueprint and you are well on your way to a stronger, better-functioning body. Release your inhibitions, your karma and emotion, and your body will be liberated from restrictions placed upon it by your unconsciousness. In this place, all things become possible.

Healing the Crystalline Earth

If you consider the massive impact the human race has had upon our wonderful Mother Earth, it is understandable that her ability to complete the final stages of the major shift in consciousness commonly known as Ascension is greatly impeded. From the clearing of her forests and the killing of her oceans, which is altering her weather and planetary self-regulatory systems, to the poisons we have introduced into her body through underground nuclear explosions, sewage and industrial toxic waste and the sprawling mass of our colossal cities, roads and urban environments that concrete, tar and pave over her skin, together with our intense emotional thoughts and actions that distort our Mother's spiritual vibration, we have imprinted a great deal upon her and she now needs as much of our loving help as we are able to give her.

This Key work can be extended to bring deep healing, cleansing and balancing to Mother Earth, to her crystalline being. The devic consciousness that supports life in the natural and mineral world within the Earth planes is perplexed as to why we have stepped so far away from a harmonious relationship with the world that supports ongoing life on the planet. Clearly we are steadily – and with increasing rapidity – killing the environment that sustains our bodies and therefore our very lives on this planet. The devas believe we have forgotten them – and to a greater extent humanity has. Without them we could not survive on Earth. Perhaps we have forgotten our true nature and ourselves. Certainly as a race we are out of balance, focusing ever more on the physical level of our consciousness, turning away from the spiritual element of our being that completes us as we use up precious natural resources on what are no more than frivolous throw-away trinkets that only amuse us for mere minutes of our existence. But as one who has remembered the devas, I can still see that all is far from lost. We must bridge across to the devic kingdoms once again and help them to support all life on Earth.

As we come closer to the major shift in consciousness, the deepest unconscious levels of our mind world are coming to the surface for release and transformation. In what appears to be the darkest of times, we are actually on the cusp of enlightenment. There is only a small ring of darkness outlining the inner light beams that are now radiating ever more strongly into this world from the spiritual planes through all life, including humanity. I am amazed at the transformations in consciousness now visibly taking place around the world. Spirituality is increasingly on the lips of many and the actions of Love are more apparent in many circles. You and I can help to strengthen that process by supporting our Mother Earth through the devas and Mineral Kingdoms in a profound way. The Keys of Creation, pure light beams that radiate directly from Source, can be used to offer healing and transformation of consciousness to our dear Mother Earth.

Instructions

This work can be undertaken in your home, in the countryside or wherever you are in the world. Making a divine relationship with Mother Earth and the over-lighting devas working with her is a profound and sacred action. This relationship, created through the Keys of Creation, will remain with you indefinitely unless you choose to surrender it by conscious choice and intention. If you choose to undertake this sacred work, please learn to walk as softly on Mother Earth as you can. Today we are asked by our governments to reduce our carbon footprint. Mother Earth asks us, in response to undertaking this healing work with her, to choose to reduce our *emotional and karmic footprint* as well. This helps us to become ever more conscious of ourselves. As we become more spiritually conscious and self aware we will choose to take deeper responsibility for ourselves and for the actions we take that affect the world environment at all levels. This of course will act to change the human world step by step and guide it towards an enlightened pathway where we will come back into balance and live harmoniously with the Earth.

Rutilated Quartz linking with the Crystal Realms

The Crystal Keys

Rose Quartz Planet

Divine Connection with Mother Earth

Prepare by centering and grounding yourself as shown on page 14.
Now link with the heart of Mother Earth and with the over-lighting devas working with Mother Earth (there is more than one over-lighting deva concerned with Mother Earth and her mineral being). Do this by taking your attention into your heart chakra.

- Feel the softness of your heart chakra and go into it

- Now go inside the soft feeling, taking your attention more deeply into the centre of your heart chakra

- Feel an even softer place right in the centre and go inside that place with your intention and awareness

- Look for the very softest feeling inside your heart chakra and take yourself there

- As you hold this soft feeling inside, place your attention on the heart of Mother Earth. Feel her soft heart and gently link with her there. Do this simply by intention. (If you are unsure about being able to do this, you can ask King Anud to help you.)

- Now become aware of the over-lighting devas that work with Mother Earth and feel their presence as you prepare to form a divine connection between you, Mother Earth and those over-lighting devas.

Whilst keeping your attention on the soft feeling in your heart chakra and Mother Earth and the devas, say:

Shek-An, Keh-Halla-An

Meh-Sha, Uurra-An

This phrase establishes a divine relationship between you, the Earth and the over-lighting devas of the Earth, creating a loving trinity with light cords between you

Take a deep breath and let go.

Feel the gentle loving cords that have formed between you, Mother Earth and the over-lighting devas who are aligned to supporting Mother Earth. This is a profound and sacred connection with Mother Earth that will remain with you unless you choose to cut those cords by intention.

Now, taking your attention fully into the softness inside your heart chakra once more, begin to recite this healing mantra slowly and repeatedly with such Love, such deep focus and in sacred connection to the divine.

Kereh-Han-Ak, Sheb, Ess-tova-An

This phrase creates a deep alignment within you to access the blueprint of the Mineral Kingdoms and for the light of the over-lighting devas aligned to Mother Earth at this level to shine their divine light through the blueprint to align Mother Earth's Mineral Kingdom more fully to the divine.

- Continue to hold this space and to repeat the mantra slowly, intuitively feeling the pace and the flow of the light of the over-lighting devas through the blueprint bringing healing to Mother Earth
- When you would like to stop, breathe deeply and gently release the focus

- Thank the over-lighting devas for the healing light, sending them your Love. Thank the Mineral Kingdoms for working with you, sending them your Love
- Hold awareness of the deep connection with Mother Earth and send her your Love and blessings, acknowledging our wonderful Mother
- When you are ready, gently withdraw

You can repeat this healing work with the over-lighting devas and the Mineral Kingdoms blueprint as often as you wish. This work is powerful, but it is perfectly safe for you and for the Earth to undertake it frequently.

We need to give a great deal in service to our Mother at this time. Her vibration is refining and she will make the shift in consciousness in due course. It is all a question of momentum – the more momentum, the faster the changes will come. The more we help our Mother to align to the divine, the more the higher planes of consciousness become accessible to her and the more easily she will unfold her Great Being.

A Note of Thanks...

I would like to thank you on behalf of the Earth and the crystals in your care for undertaking the healing work that has been laid out in this book. I cannot stress enough the fundamental importance of holding divine alignment and working with the deepest possible divine connection in all that you do at this time. As we move more deeply in to the major shift in consciousness now taking place, the fear and the resistance we all feel intensifies to unprecedented levels. If we allow the fear to take root within us, what we create will not be our highest choice. It is the choices we make on a day-to-day basis that are creating this world right now. Your healing contribution at the highest level you can sustain both for yourself and for the Earth helps to make this world a much better place.

Appendices

Tables Summarising Anaritas Techniques

The following tables summarise the Anaritas light language steps contained in the various tools and techniques in this book to help you work with them more easily.

Please Note
The tables do not give complete information on using the tools. It is important to become thoroughly familiar with the crystal and blueprint techniques before using the tables as a reference. Remember that the techniques require certain attitudes and sacred relationship positions to be held with yourself and the crystalline structures whilst uttering the Anaritas phrases.

If you have not worked with the techniques for a while and may have forgotten some of the steps, please refer to the relevant sections in the book for complete information before continuing your work.

Table 1: Cleansing, Divine relationship, Core essence

Anaritas Phrase	Description
Veh-Reh-Shua, Eh-San, Eh-San	Cleansing crystals - can be repeated up to three times
Shek-An, Keh-Halla-An Meh-Sha, Uurra-An	Creates a divine relationship between you, your crystal and the over-lighting deva of your crystal
Varishar-An, Ney-At Ku-Rashua-An-At Kereh-Halla-An, Eh-San, Eh-San	Enables the crystal to commune deeply with the Mineral Kingdom and to receive blessings
Kreh-Halla-An, Cru-Ak, Eh-San Kuru-Shella-An, Eh-San, Eh-San	Reveals the core essence of the crystal, its root programming and enables the crystal to radiate this core quality

Table 2: Programming and Meditating with Crystals

Anaritas Phrase	Description
Programming a Crystal	
Varu-Ka-An, "programme" Eh-San, Eh-San	Cleanse crystal before using this phrase. Choose programme carefully in accordance with your divine relationship with your crystal
Meditation and Illumination with Crystals	
Acra-An-Nu, Sharac-Anash-An-Nu	Opens a pathway between you, your crystal and the over-lighting deva of your crystal. Opens gateways to crystalline consciousness and unconditional Love, uniting you with aspects of Source for meditation and illumination

Table 3: Healing Through Your Body Etheric Blueprint

Anaritas Phrase	Description
Preparation:	Complete grounding, cleansing and aligning work with your body as shown in **Table 1** above. Place the palms of your hands over the heart and navel chakras
Sherak-Ka-Han, Shellath, Sherat **Ah-Han, Han-Nu**	Cleanses and balances the etheric blueprint of your body in preparation for healing through the blueprint
	Hold awareness of the over-lighting deva who oversees your physical body crystalline structure standing in front of you and sending loving devic life-supporting energy to you. At the same time, hold awareness of your etheric blueprint surrounding your physical body. Intend to direct the over-lighting devic energies through your etheric blueprint. Allow their light patterns to shine deeply through your physical body into every crystalline molecular structure of your body. In this way you are gently re-programming your body in accordance with divine will, enabling it to adopt the patterning of perfect form and beingness ... /

Repeat the two phrases below slowly as a mantra for a period of time	
Arass, Cru-Ak, Kerrah-Alla-An **Eh-San, Eh-San**	Feel the life-sustaining patterns radiating into your physical body through the etheric blueprint. Feel the involvement of the over-lighting devas invoked through the Anaritas light language. Visualise the high vibration divine light of the over-lighting devic energy shining brightly through the etheric blueprint and visualise this soft soothing light radiating deeply into your body tissue, molecular and crystalline structure.
Meh-ha-ta **Seh-An, Seh-An**	Temporarily releases the emotional overlays that your torment and fear have layered into the physical body. This will allow the natural re-patterning of the etheric blueprint light structure to reach deeply into the crystalline structure of the physical body uninterrupted by emotional and belief-system overlays, whilst the energy work is taking place.

Table 4: Healing the Earth

Centre and ground yourself.
Link with the heart of Mother Earth and with the over-lighting devas working with Mother Earth. - Look for the softest feeling inside your heart chakra and take yourself there - As you hold this soft feeling inside, place your attention on the heart of Mother Earth. Feel her soft heart and gently link with her. Now become aware of the over-lighting devas that work with Mother Earth and feel their presence as you prepare to form a divine connection between you, Mother Earth and the over-lighting devas.

Anaritas Phrase	Description
Shek-An, **Keh-Halla-An** **Meh-Sha, Uurra-An**	Establishes a divine relationship between you, the Earth and the over-lighting devas of the Earth, creating a loving trinity with light cords between you … /

Kereh-Han-Ak, Sheb Ess-tova-An	Then recite the following healing mantra slowly and repeatedly with such Love, such deep focus and in sacred connection to the divine. **Creates a deep alignment within you to access the blueprint of the Mineral Kingdoms and for the light of the over-lighting devas aligned to Mother Earth at this level to shine their divine light through the blueprint to align Mother Earth's Mineral Kingdom more fully to the divine.** Continue to hold this space and to repeat the mantra slowly, intuitively feeling the pace and the flow of the light of the over-lighting devas through the blueprint. When you would like to stop, breathe deeply and gently release the focus. Thank the over-lighting devas for the healing light, sending them your Love. Thank the Mineral Kingdoms for working with you, sending them your Love. Hold awareness of the deep connection with Mother Earth and send her your Love and blessings, acknowledging our wonderful Mother. Then gently withdraw.